T0083860

Missing

the Moon

Also by Bin Ramke

Missing
the Moon

Bin Ramke

OMNIDAWN PUBLISHING
RICHMOND, CALIFORNIA
2014

© Copyright Bin Ramke 2014. All rights reserved.

Cover photos courtesy of NASA photo archive

Book cover and interior design by Peter Burghardt

Offset printed in the United States
by Edwards Brothers Malloy, Ann Arbor, Michigan
On 55# Enviro Natural 100% Recycled 100% PCW
Acid Free Archival Quality FSC Certified Paper
with Rainbow FSC Certified Colored End Papers

Library of Congress Cataloging-in-Publication Data

Ramke, Bin, 1947-
  [Poems. Selections]
  Missing the moon / Bin Ramke.
      pages ; cm
  ISBN 978-1-63243-000-7 (pbk. : alk. paper)
  I. Title.
  PS3568.A446A6 2014
  811'.54--dc23

                                    2014013749

Published by Omnidawn Publishing, Richmond, California
www.omnidawn.com   (510) 237-5472   (800) 792-4957
          10 9 8 7 6 5 4 3 2 1
          ISBN: 978-1-63243-000-7

CONTENTS

3   Pronouncing the Asterisk

for Linda and Nic

If I ever. When the moon of mourning
is set and gone.

Finnegans Wake

Part One: The Inconceivable

It is to this method of subjecting everywhere infinity to algebraical calculations, that the name is given of differential calculations or of fluxions and integral calculation. It is the art of numbering and measuring exactly a thing whose existence cannot be conceived.

And indeed, would you not imagine that a man laughed at you who should declare that there are lines infinitely great which form an angle infinitely little?

Voltaire, *Letters on the English*, XVII

CONTAIN

Like tiny dandelions down the page
the devices wander marking edges
but the page is paler than blown seeds
against the moon, watch:
contain is what a body does
until it doesn't, and spills itself.

NO PLACE YOU'VE BEEN

Climb up on the moon? Of course we did. All you had to do
was to row out to it in a boat and, when you were underneath,
prop a ladder against her and scramble up.
                    "The Distance of the Moon," Italo Calvino

Concave reflections make flat worlds
larger, more loved than the thing—
reflection; who has not climbed mirrored
into himself in the morning?
Musingly magnified his face
floating above water?

At the water hole animals gather reflective
at dusk, Africa on Sunday evening TV;
the endearing giraffe splay-legged over
an image of giraffe drinking, sister image—
A garden inclosed is my sister,

my spouse; a spring shut up, a fountain
sealed (Song of Songs 4:12) —asymptote—
another symptomatic morning
after the night of rain—a night
of random rain.

I wanted to watch clouds arrive
after drought but they came in the night
thiefish then fled at the light.
I awoke it was only
today not yet

tomorrow I will again awaken
into a day still folded waiting
like laundry for use. I wanted
to name clouds arriving
a function of time

and topography, clouds a curl of air
and water over mountains clouds
like lenses through which
to watch the wavery
end of a season.

*

Someone entered our city
under cover of umbrella, the first,
of many the last to linger he
learned a new language he
came to say to stay, stray.

*

Daily I stroll contentedly in my garden
There is a gate, but it is always shut.   (Tao Yuanming)
Plants produce organic stuff
from inorganic matter; animals don't.
Animals die of lack. A tiny world
teems with anguish, with narrow
stems through which fluids flow
topped by gorgeous, outlandish …
flowers.

A bloom is a blessing because.
Was the gate blessing or curse
was the gate protection or denial
was it a gate (hand through)
or a door (hand against)

a thousand grasses under my feet
I walk in despair or in ecstasy crushing
that which cannot move.
The smells of a garden include filth
which resides in the mind, mingles
like Adam and his wife hid
themselves from the presence

13

of the Lord God amongst the trees
of the garden. Genesis 3:8

*

Laika travelled farthest of any dog and suffered
as animals do a lonely death in the modern mode:
the day before launch Yazdovsky brought her home
to play with his children—animal among animals
the next day encased in a capsule, traveller trapped

A garden inclosed is my sister, my spouse;
a spring shut up, a fountain sealed.
This difference, animals
from human animals: plants
from inorganic matter we made
from it. Rockets and random places.
Teem with anguish, with narrow
stems through which fluids flow.
Happy the hare, lucky the leaf.

"Happy the hare at morning, for she cannot read
The Hunter's waking thoughts. Lucky the leaf
Unable to predict the fall."   (W. H. Auden)

Gorgeous outland, earth
animals die of, dearth,
tiny world of privation
in (curious word) space.

MOON AND AUTUMN GRASSES (TAWARAYA SŌTATSU, d.1640)

A preamble along this shore this evening,
—the principle of maximum ignorance—
as darkness crept cleverly close.

Closeness our constant condition, we said *modern*
but didn't mean what it meant. We meant *recent*.
We meant *us*. I am like you, deferent.

Like lovers we didn't object
to wandering, would wend
wend and wind; and wand. Join
me and wind (verb?

noun?) back at the beach:
I know your lovable qualities.
I have a theory of calculus and time.

   *

To calculate place a spot on the beach relative to
some thing which recalculates its own position
stones on the sand, impressions
relative to: Footprint. Ghost crab. Stray dog.
Common gateway interface. A place, our place.

We made words together.
We discovered a lost word,
purlewe (land on the edge of a forest),
from *puralee*, French *pur-* (thoroughly) + *aler* (to go).

Under the light of the night
the whiteness of the eye lies
always open behind lids and liquids,
tears and terrors.

   *

Nothing can be said safely
—recall courting, flirting:
I made claims, often wrong;
I being wrong started new futures.

                *

Is the moon a silvery streak in water?
The moon was a silvered disk,
a Japanese moon on a painted
field a folding screen the moon
pure silver become corrosion
after two hundred years a black smear
art thwarted to black; to black from sulfur
in the air of, the reflective moon in the mind
of some painter defeated by the elemental.
Selenium, a nonmetal, often replaces sulfur
in metal sulfide ores. Selenium was named for the moon
as tellurium was named for earth.

                *

We call this an asterisk but I want moons
on the page to mark change like day
to night, month to next month, time not space;

precision is a way to separate
space from time. One second
of arc a degree of precision
but spherical excess means a shape
will not close if calculated on a plane
then measured on the earth's surface.
Under moonlight the earth is big
the mountainous moon, small.

I leave a track with pen, ink,
a corrosive trail of intent.

The reflective liquids know more
than the dark. There is a trail
left by the snail in the garden tonight.

OF THE VEGETATIVE NIGHT

A word can contain terrors
readily as rotting logs leak legs, centipedes
and caterpillars. Back to home. Travel was
torture. And work. Travail.

the world around it is like a mine where the precious green
vein finds everything necessary for the continual   ("Fauna and Flora"
elaborations of its protoplasm,   Francis Ponge)

we are fuel frantic to outrace the fire
we are the fire
we sleep through it, if we live
long enough we live;
however, soon we don't

                    *

spring is a reminder is a local issue
like certain politics and the news
slow burning then fast

                    *

Sometimes the plant sometimes the caterpillar
catches the eye. Vigorous feeders turning
other into self. A neat trick, how one day's
hand is the next day's glove.

At night the plants
hear each other in Latin, the names
on the labels ... readable in morning light.

*

Like tiny dandelions down the page
the devices wander marking edges
but the page paler than blown seeds
against the moon, watches.
Contain is what a body does
until it docsn't, then spells itself.

LOCALLY EUCLIDIAN

Waterfall

Scelsi stopped composing around 1975, but enjoyed belated fame as musicians from all over the world discovered his work

Via San Vita, Valva, where at the moment a line of green laundry
occludes the view—but we are passersby and see into gardens,
slovenly terraces cumulous with cast-off furniture, leggy Ligustrums,
tinted terrazzo. All with its gorgeous echoing viva voce
around some corner. But we are going to swim

My brother loved swimming. Bayous and beaches,

underwater making a tube of water into which a self

I never learned his skill to exit gracefully

I walk out of rooms as a way to stop talking

I ignore telephones as a way out of friendships

                    *

The most astonishing concept—a water fall—
in *this* flat country, this land of long views.
But from beneath the river the swimmer did hear
the threat of the edge of the world, the corner
downward turned by the water, the crashing below.

Or was this a dream, he in his darkness
damp with fearful future. There is a river
or two within, blood and endocrine rivulets
falling and churning. He was a child and
no child should suffer dark without and within.

Butterflies are known to drink the tears
of children along riverbanks—salt and similar
hormonal secretions attract the metamorphic
species. A child of empire, helpless
little leaflet floating just beneath the surface.

Forest rivers fascinate, beguile by being two worlds
both dangerous. As of overlapping centuries
we belong in neither, tree nor water, air nor
rock. He heard sounds but turned to the piano

to interiors; child of Empire, taught the sound
to sit up, to speak, to beg. He would touch
one key with one finger again and again
hours at a time, then sleep, then again

to cure himself he said. But I was thinking
of myself, my days along rivers among the trees
wholly within the sounds and airs of anger,
of angels of heat, insects and other stinging.

Nor was it the history of water I was recalling
nor was it music, the making of a note.

A paper image of water is possible: it could be glassine,
or a poem. A poem is always an image of water, a shape-
less containing, or shapely. Old English *gesceap* (listen—
you can hear it forming). A consistency elegant of loss,
water engages the mind. I did look at landscapes, the

small museum we made at art class. I tried to indicate
water with upside-down trees, cypress, wiggly. And blue
pastel even though the water was brown. But my teacher
had tricks and I learned some, tricks for depicting water.
In spite of water as container, always, for example

*The aim of this study is to register the presence of aquatic insects during the
rainy and dry seasons, in 15 dune lakes of the Gulf of Mexico's coastal zone.*

Meeting the Orphan

Order of Chivalry 31: Thoffyce of a knyght is to mayntene
and deffende wymmen widowes and orphan   (Caxton)

the orphan is coming!   I am leaving to meet her
she will arrive early   before the dew has dried
she will be watching   for me, she will
worry if I am not there to greet

Scelsi experienced a neurotic break during which
"I forgot everything I ever knew about music";
to soothe his mind he played single notes over and over on the piano,
a form of self-therapy which became
his mature compositional practice.

I will be earlier than this   earlier than anyone I
will bring gifts and consolation

I will be too late no matter   how early I leave this
is the nature of orphan   of orphan the nature is
how early I leave this   matter, it will ever be late

later it will be that there is orphanage, not a place a condition
of mind of old people orphans all

I will help her I will   the widow the woman
I her orphan no matter who

imagine a drip, say, from a limestone ceiling
at a rate unchanged millennia at a time

I have come to imagine that my attraction to water is an attraction to
reflections. To imagine is to put into pictures, to understand in and
as image. I have come to the images of images. My childhood was
watery, full of wavery houses and trees and clouds and faces. The
water was slow moving or still—swamps lakes bayous coulees and
ditches puddles buckets empty tires overturned. These were waters
to breed, to nurture larvae: mosquitoes mayflies dragonflies.

I made no music I made images

There was history like a waterfall heard from beneath
lines leading there the pull of grave water still there was time
to reach the shore to stand on two feet on land perpendicular
to the pull of the river and walk into ignorance happy
if still wet and now the mosquitoes.

*There were not significant differences in the alpha diversity within the same
lake during the two climatic seasons. The trophic structure is dominated by
the detritivorous groups (57% of scrapers, collectors, gatherers, shredders),
followed by predators (38%) and herbivores (5%).*

I do remember the strange eloquent angles
of herons. As if reading poems,
walking stiffly, stabbing through surface
at imagery below. As day died into night
the glitter of small fish slipped down the gullet
to die at some point into bird, fish to bird,
into flight, escaping the waterfall

even though air vibrates to the fall of water
to the thudding fall of water on rock relentless.

PICNIC AMONG STRANGERS

Spring leaves green and birds back cackling
among the thorns and blaring sun. A day a day.
The time has come sprung upon us
to gather again small humans among
large mountains.

Our thin thinking varies: some
consider the colors of the map, how many
and where the borders touch and whether
a corner counts. Some make machines to think

a thing or two. Some tremble. Obsessive
observers watch each other and pounce
upon occasion. Occasionally converge. Sit opposite
each other hauntingly chewing.

Conversation: we could see a word shared
required at dinner. It seemed to mean
meanness, contrary verse—turn with or turn
against. Families fight, we told ourselves.

Conversely we turned together against
The Others, those away, those awash in the world.
Every planar map can be colored with at most
four colors. Everyone knew already.

There came forth dogs from the house
three together followed curves of pursuit
toward and then past

then silence followed and a day
reflected a previous day.

Contradiction as the path most admittedly
the way out. To speak against as to speak above;
shouting became the proof most general.
Spring forward, fall back.

And as four colors does suffice,
any map imaginable brings us home
if home is various enough widely
ranged against mountainous
possibility, particolored and
pretentious, pretended, imagined.

MEAN ALSO MEANS

By a *predicabile* Albertus Magnus means:
a thing of which something is or can be said.
I Ching says:
A bird takes flight, leaving its call behind.

Fortune means telling, tallying
the means of profit, of prophesy.

Here we are again, aging
against each other. There was one
once who made just and gentle plans.
This was in the time of the birth
of the gods. Meaning came later,
meanness.

Part Two: Phases of the Earth

We went into darkness after being in daylight the whole time on the way to the Moon. And then we went into darkness. And were in the shadow [...] of the Moon.

Eugene Cernan

CURVE OF PURSUIT

A point, a line, alignment. Lovely
the lingering along the shore
as the century lies in wait:

hunger and indiscretion.
I am one of many, or not even one,
but am of many one who watches waves

and allows particulate sand its say:
say, its sound, susurrant. Of many one
engaging the ear as if the Pacific

meant its name, as if the edge of
continent contented us with boundary.
Draw a line from A to B. Live there.

POPULATION GENETICS

Family: we gathered our tomato stakes from the casket factory;
I learned to carve basswood from the prosthesis maker—
he let me gather scraps I turned into birds and small
animals of the order *Rodentia*.

The timid species of humans would wander and
at night could hear twigs snapping along paths, hear
a murmur of clothes against their thighs. The nights stayed
warm in those days, and the moonlight continuous.
I never saw such a time but I know

a time before memory. There was a time the oxygen
was so plentiful six-limbed creatures could for a cost
burn brighter; they learned to fly and live short lives
during a time the forests would easily flame, sap crackle
enthusiastic into filaments filling the nights
filling the days with smoke

then percentages altered, nitrogen gathered
while tiny creatures survived the flame
airborne learning to pierce
the skin of mammals, to burn the blood of others;

I carve my creatures to live in my own light air.

A RANDOM WALK

She grew there, up, among plants
and images, insects, sex, and such.
Animals to serve her, here, served

a mind most attached, to be attached —
look how lovely love is, the humidity
and the shape of the leaf (sword shape)

and the shade it cast, palmetto. If I
could I would bring "green" into the poem.
Five hundred and ten nanometers

right in the middle of the visible spectrum.
Specter. The green of palmetto darkened
with depth into the swamp she waded

into a kind of danger not very but still
there were snakes and sex, insects
and there was the growing to do.

Those leaves, those palmetto fronds
would wave in wind, would cut flesh.
Kepler was the first to use "focus"

for a geometrical shape, the spot
where rays come together, as sun
formed into fire a hazard by boys .

around ant beds. Her adventures
were bucolic, leisurely, greenly
gathering among wildlife

an occasional orchid (a keen
eye needed to find it, but there
it could be), curious testament.

HAPPY IS HE WHO HAS DISCOVERED THE CAUSES OF THINGS

Whoever. Ancient. I did
love their words, and do, still,
today, spring, the season being all of *now* I need,

ancient spring but the smell a present, only
present. They named the season for being first, arising
like water from the rock…source. To them, *ver*, a word

in Latin but Melbancke wrote *In vear, the husbandman lop*
their trees, to the intent that afterward they may growe
the better while now I prune the apple and

remember crape myrtle, azalea, camellia, jasmine, all
abloom by now back there
all fill a mind with nearness.

But an airplane passes. I hear it. And various drones
that mean a kind of being — the vacuum cleaner,
the floor polisher, also flies and bees

and a distant ocean, an interstate,
a mother's sewing machine, sounds,
the electric typewriter from one's past

switched on, waiting. The ceiling fan.
The blood circulates mindless
of the season, the smell, the inner ear.

A MOLECULAR VISION CLOUDED

If it is true that Velazquez
intended the exposed weave of canvas
to indicate brickwork in the wall of the Jardin
de la Villa Medicis in Rome, then how
modern! of him to allow the thing itself

to shine through simulation.

Can you hear a future?
No, it is only vision.

*

An interest in the life span
of clouds informed his vision
of the impossible (the old use
of *shine*, to be transparent —

through paint the canvas shines; or,
the paint is thin stuff,
it shines through)

Can you see a future?
No, it is shiny.

*

Do you know Velazquez's *The Forge of Vulcan*?
A piece of iron glows orange
or seems to—in Abbeville I would watch

my uncle at his forge make metal glow
and what would shine would be turned
and twisted into use.

But it seemed to me I could see
through iron into the source of shine, atomic.

AFTER AUDUBON

I would speak of ferocity,
the hummingbird—the needling
fear invoked, the pain of petals the sugared attack
we watched blood collect, ruby drops
a good proportion of all she had

defending self or territory. A mind more
small more swift to anger, if anger is what
provokes, if mind matters. Arvo Pärt
is playing, a sound from the house

as we on the balcony watch floral agonies, a world
proceeding beneath us,
contemptuous of us, comfortable
enough. *Spiegel im spiegel*, we said to the bird
gone, she of the blood-glitter of sun

small thing small thinker. It is a bird named for a sound,
named for its own wings' accidental effects.
To be named for the sound you make, Poet,
without intent, without meaning.

"weaponized pastoral"

Light moss along the north
   sides the trees boy scout lore
      the handbook the brilliance

these trees nearby mines
   abandoned arsenic, zinc,
      cadmium, copper,

Peru Creek, seven
   thousand abandoned mines
      Animas River devoid

cast out all aquatic life
   I do not know this
      I am a visitor

you loved me once
   anyway, left a little
      for the next in line

but looked only up to
   the sky when the sky
      was its blackest

and polished telescopes
   fiddled with settings
      photographed Jupiter,

photographed Mars and
   stars amid galaxies
      spinning like hard drives

like wheels within
   wheels, problems
      of distance and time

But as I have shown, this world is not made of solid body,
   since there is void intermingled in things; nor yet
      is it like the void De Rerum Natura, 5-365

we deal with body last
   because it has a surface, is first
      to know its own shape

like a breast which yields
   when asked by mouth
      the mouth and leaking breath

a tongue which takes a shape
   of an interior (think water)
      the lips and teeth and lungs,

alveoli, larynx, sphenoid sinuses,
   secret, silent adolescent …
      those who search the mouths

of lovers for something
   with the tongue, a Braille un-
      translatable, unlearned

others who listen in the night
   for the dream speech
      of the beloved who answer,

to become one in her dream,
   trying to trap her there
      one will open eyes as if

to force a seeing, a sight
   to force it into the brain
      to take a shape of thought

which is not yet thought, does
   not belong to lovers
      is no one's tool or toy

or task, a last prime
   among the mysteries
      so much smaller so

divisible by itself and one
   but the Frenchman said
      if you laugh

it is because you are afraid;
   if you are afraid it is
      spring and floral;

fear has a botanical component
   Frenchmen fear flowers
      while Americans fear

minerals, heavy metals, flow
   of their own effluvia down
      stream land of little-leafed

flora; she was afraid
   to ask for details, for
      explanations of flowers near for

a map of secrets,
   secretions of the earth
      sounding like weather.

MATTERING

after an image by Sarah Walko

out of gloom uncoiling
yet the lines are straight in a locally Euclidean sort of way
the shape of a kite compels geometry
the measure of the earth the earth of measurement
being still   so far for so available a being
still in broken and disguised patterns
o so broken we have become
we always were so, broken, becoming

a beautiful a blue   a sky blue sky
remember watery sky blushing
into dark continuous twilight two lights
are better than none   uncoiling a
kite straight string

out of gloom uncoiling a gorgeous need
I like lines rulers ruling the paper
the point of o perspective if you like
like if you speculate a point of
departure order a point of blue in
the kite shaped sky through windows
windowing a world winnow a world

how wide a lake a
single cloud might make,
how blue a shape

I knew the mind of a boy as a place but
disorderly but minded his manners his
matter he was blue and seemed to have
a shape like a soap film within intersect-
ing sticks as if any polygon could think
imagine he was more beautiful than ice
you had to be where there was weather
in there and moons too and a prim
    cloud of primes—twins twining.

IN LATE EVENING THE LIGHT OVERSEEN

She had this done: a small flock,
birds tattooed on her body only
by friends seen, a few birds
visible;

imagine her as that
that no longer exists erased
by the hand of the artist, thumb
rubbed

like graphite on paper except
it is flesh that feels
pain inflecting infecting her
reading

of his writing, the artist
who said I love the word *little*
as the needle
dripped

ink with which the artist
wrote replied I mainly
quote Vonnegut,
Everything

was beautiful and nothing hurt
the motto of modern tattooing
or so it goes
it

is mostly about healing
there are scars where
she made him
erase

A body a boy, born
on his skin verses appeared
from Qur'an
lingered a day or two then left

in Moscow one explained it
as illusion, one as illness
some showed with beet juice how
it could be done

or red wine and henna
sometimes the verses misspelled
Oh errors fleshed miraculous
an eros carving a way in skin

researchers found among prisoners
self-inflected among the ill prisoners solitary;
summary statistical: cut own skin
burned with cigarette burned with match
carved words into skin
carved pictures
purposely scratched self until bled
broke skin with sandpaper
dropped acid on skin spilled
bleach oven cleaner
sharp object fallen onto
shards of plastic of glass of pottery
rubbed on until into skin
broke own bones

Ornithographia: the reading
of talon scratches on skin
of escaped prey

ALL IS DIVISIBLE AND INDIVISIBLE

They do not apprehend how being at variance it
agrees with itself

There is a connection working in both directions,
as in the bow and the lyre: now argument resumes.

Violence begets a verb or will when writing resumes:

The boy walks into the woods

The girl walks out of the woods

the lyrical arc of the arrow determined, demented
as an imagined fate or fault

the lyre became every plucked instrument
then they are glad because they be quiet, he quoted.

Sound seems logarithmic, as
in: increasing by decibels, by
tens and hundreds. I want to
crowd the light, this one life
leaving us speedily, spilling
by tens and hundreds like blood
from every wound, wind and
ignition—light leaves first
as in Genesis. Arrival of sound
after—see thunder. *See*

The miraculous builds in cities
because of all the mirroring;
modern cities; glass and polished
metal an agony of glimmered
sheen, reflective: how many
of those faces I pass can really
be me?

Two kings of India approached a
tree. One claimed to know exactly
the number of leaves on the tree.
The other, to prove him wrong, tore
off leaves from the tree, counting by
ones. But as he destroyed, other leaves
fell naturally, and other leaves erupted
and some leaves are also blooms and
should not be counted. The first
king proceeded into the forest while the
second king is still counting, even today.

HAUSDORFF SPACES

It was like being inside a parachute
after landing—assuming survival—
the collapsing textures with light
shining through and the rotating
earth beneath you benign again.
He said. He had been loved.

A separation axiom, he said, has nothing
to do with love. Metrization, o love,
turns distance into desire, space into
place without distance. She is there
I am here but there, he explained,
being bounded but not totally bounded.

But to be above yet falling, to be falling yet
to be unafraid, to be unafraid yet to know
reasons for fear, to be secure in knowledge
yet to respect ignorance as a kind of home:

This is not a lecture, he said, it is lunch.
He reached across her hands for wine
to pour for her, for her alone in her neighborhood.

GOING WITHOUT, SAYING

Played with magnets watched one spin when
held against the other north to north like repels
like night to day

it is light—there is light now visible—no
night is going, elsewhere shadowed

in morning light a morning glory
morning face insects to dine there, thereon—slenderer
messages sent against fasting far ranging
arranging daylight against green of grass and all

when I see the flower stem bend with the weight
of the bee I know what to believe every
emperor clothed the shell of the thing flying
from the thing into the eye is belief. My eye.

SOLVE GENERAL BOUNDARY VALUE PROBLEMS

(Hilbert's twentieth problem, an elegy)

Incompleteness is a gift; boundaries engage and gather.
There are rules to this life, this little languishing between
space and other space. The beautiful child returned
from the fields full of anguish, the child undaunted,
the child unanguished. Untamed. Tender of heart.

The field she explored was a Moore-neighborhood moving
around her, a shadow self-cast in all directions: no sun
sufficed. No wolf entered to threaten or to thrive.
To be a child is to heal the center emptied by
one's own birth. It is a puzzle, public and pitiable.
There are solutions to every set, every sun, Sol.

To have a child is to pose the problem. Solve
for X. For Y. Forever. When a thing is next
to another thing, is there a between thing,
and what shall we feed it, when will it be tamed?
Undaunted we discover a language in the weeds

low-level language of topology
Point-set topology, set-theoretic topology (general)
the study of the general abstract nature of continuity
        or closeness on spaces. Consider
any family, distances define. Between any two
members a third may intervene; the measure
of closeness is casualty, causality.

Continuity, dimension, compactness, connectedness:
Intermediate Value Theorem: if a path in the real line

a path between brother and brother shall we say
      connects two members, then it passes over every
      point between the two;

Euclidean n-space is homeomorphic to
      Euclidean m-space iff m=n
in other words when my brother died my father was already
dead my mother soon to follow. All have similar stories
in the end, those not already orphaned. We
have words for equal: similar: homeomorphic. None
are what we mean them to mean;

here is a question: "When can a topology on a space
be derived from a metric?" I could see only surface
no matter how deeply I dug—all I could expose
was surface, even of water, even of blood.
Or do we see into the body of water? When he drowned
did the touching interiors, body and water, mean?

Continuities compared, their properties explored
inquiry into the geometrical properties of spaces and
continuous functions between spaces

he did not drown he lives in air

algebraic topology: study of intrinsic qualitative
aspects of spatial objects all are objects in space
even memory lives on surfaces electrical surfaces,
spheres, tori, circles, knots, links, configuration spaces

continuous one-to-one (homeomorphic)
transformations rubber-sheet topology
different kinds of hole structures
hole structures often best represented by groups, rings
(algebraic objects) hole structures, as in continuous space
you have made in the world by living a life, any life,
all lives lived homeomorphic to a worm's way made
through substance, eating dirt which opens
the way under obstacles, leaving the leavings behind.

Hole structures: if nothing can have a structure
then anything can and does and is a poem.

RULE OF DOUBLE FALSE POSITION

There will be morning, and there will be evening
and between is the life lived, leaving out the darker hours.

A life in the light as a burden, as a cost, a calculus
of straight-edged shadows. Of blinking into the sun.

A science of vision was once upon a time
how to paint pictures, how to draw, how to

remember the small shadows of a face. Fact.
(But what IS the probability that a random chord

of a circle is larger than the side of an inscribed
equilateral triangle? Not the answer but the asking

can make a life in the light.) Evening as in
leveling, rounding the corners, softening

the edges. It is evening now and he thinks
he sees the child he was or loved among

the leaves, some shrubbery or other whose green
substitutes for night, whose interior could hide

any number of small animals or children
peering out calculatingly.

TRADITIONAL FUTURE: A TENSE

She promised her mother she'd be home by puberty
but the times do change, the expectations and the frippery
of culture, and besides, it would be too late by then any
way, any Tao. How could we hope

to raise young humans to be other than they want
to be. By "we" I mean those left at the lapping edge
of the future, people of the beach, watching for
some sail to see if it is black or back at all.

Here is what numbers were: A group of people
buy hens together. Each person contributes 8 *wen*, and 3
wen are left over; 7 are contributed, and 4 is the deficit.
How many people, and

what is the cost of the hens? *Chiu Chang Suan Shu*
(*Nine Chapters on the Mathematical Art*). My personal
favorite is the paradox of material implication; as they
say, *ex contradictione sequitur quodlibet*.

Speaking in the traditional future subjunctive she
promised to be home, and home she was in time
if not on time. It was a new world, where farms are
server farms, cost Google millions

per month to cool—the principle of explosion proves
everything, she said to me that evening, both of us
avoiding the ghost crabs, admiring the squadrons
of pelicans cruising, lusting

after the dolphin displays, the play of splash and glitter
in the setting sun. See, there is life there yet, yet
being ambiguous. And yet. People live here,
you'd be amazed, the Poet wrote.

MY PRIVATE PERIODIC TABLE

The first-ever affinity table, (table des rapports), which was based on displacement reactions, was published in 1718 by Étienne-François Geoffroy

1
I prefer an aesthetic
of future feeling in the act
of passing: in other words, a present

to the self to come. In other
words, words written, to be read
later—a tabular ignorance blind

burdens borne wildly spurned
then picked up by passersby
by stranger selves to come, late selves.

"The present moment lasts
three seconds," Holub wrote,
more or less. I, no less

a child than you, we
competed for our presents
three seconds at a burst, energetic

elementals. Remember the morning
we met in the mirrored
metallics, like fish rising

to lures, rules against the light
lingering too low on that artificial
horizon, home. ... work

at it however hard, never
will the moment move
however snail-paced back.

2
Symmetries, groups,
kids in a ring chanting
profanity: but time afflicts
the fumbled future, too;
the present we made up
to succumb to a warm day,
a warning day to day
a cry wolfish among us —
a farm to pass a summer in
where hay warmed wet
in the barn
then burst

forth brilliant element
a malignant mineral
glitter

3
Chemistry conceals—see light
leak between words, any words
adjacent: leave gaps, glowing—

Plumbago for your pencil,
a penny for any thoughts,
mineral ministries—the fields

lay fallow, hallowed
even when we
wrote it

down: the metal the
regulus the ores the
earths minus phlogiston

made metals. There were rules.
We all got chemistry sets
for Christmas

each to mix
futures alone
among the elements.

4
In 1789 thirty-three
choices from which a simple
world was made.

Here is my new list: Time,
Space, Number, Child, Dog,
Stranger, Danger.

Danger itself creates a world—
infection, for instance: teeming
world within a wound.

Enduring endearing pain—
new items for my list:
Pain and Dust.

Oh, and Mirror,
the act not the thing,
new elements, old cures (curse).

DISQUIET

    Is as If

Light is a place to start.

Light as a place

to start an agony of particles

wavering. Quiver.

Vafra, "flicker." Old Norse.

To allow to become a waif, that is,
to abandon … waiver

late Middle English: from an Anglo-Norman
French variant of Old Northern French *gaif*, probably
of Scandinavian origin. Early use was often in *waif and
stray*, as a legal term denoting a piece of property found
and, if unclaimed, falling to the lord of the manor.

There Was an Apple; Was There Poison

when the body was found there was nearby
an apple, and in the body was cyanide
and there was a witch and a forest and dwarves

All He Knows Are Names

when the plane banked the glare
against the eyelid shaped a curve
of light catenary

her neck and shoulder formed

she leaned one shoulder bare
the drape, enough, awake
a thread across a void

He travels to a new world
his machine in mind
his oracle to consult.

A Machine for Answers

who speaks, who says from home
I am not at home—whose voice
is not the answer—my voice
I am not from where I say
an echo voiceless placeless
bodiless a poem
air provoked a man
wanders this way waiting.

(for the centenary of the birth of Alan Turing)

THE CHEMICAL BASIS OF MORPHOGENESIS

In spite of the season in
the center is heat enough
to kill but nothing
lives there. Still, we
spin above it, skaters or
insects taking to water,
talking to water, thin ice.

*

In a mountainous region cows
below the campanile crop the grass
listening or not to their own bell sounds scattered
—stillness shattered, still

change-ringing the morning
the alarm—awake a weakening
listening as if to snow
but snow now damps

the vibratory world the very
rocks ringing, would ring
otherwise. Weather.

*

The century is arbitrary, still
many were born a hundred
years ago, most now gone
the glamorous grammar of time

the accidence of fall as season
(*O God it is Time, lay your shadows*   (Rilke)
across the sundial, obscure obscure)
cover, cover, recover

with snow or any scatter
leaflike and softly corrupting.

*

We are each the shape it took:
the smell of thyme still rises
from underfoot, like sacrifice
to an ancient sense, a sensory god
greedy and of my own making.

We have a gland, thymus (not thyroid)
which worked before birth then slowed
at puberty; it is deeply a part of each
apart from the heart yet there under
guardian ribs weakly works to keep us.

We are little chemistry sets, we leak
lyrical and lifelike.

*

A page can be as snow but
water is water, the wet page weeps ink
sinking into the silent obscure.

Or sand: sand is dry, can be.
White with light and susurrous.

Sound of the thinnest silence.

Daughter of sound, voice of, too.

The breath obstructed becomes the poem.

The bent men cross in front of the preacher
and all acknowledge such primacy, prim

engagement of limb with limb, pain
straightens the knee, bends the back

against recovery. They made no sound
nor left a track, like deer to the dark-edged.

*

How thin the air which enables sound—we can climb almost to its loss, the breath and the word compete when the climber attains the summit: quiet emotion and lack of oxygen.

*

Air takes its shape from gravity, its edge.

Part Three: Pronouncing the Asterisk

I am but a small noise I have several noises in me
Tristan Tzara

RESONANCE

In 1938 John Cage composed a piece for the U.C.L.A. swimming
team's annual water-ballet. Because vibrations through air are
impeded by water, Cage experi-mented with gongs, lowered into
the water, which could be heard by the swimmers.

To hear voices means to hear not-voices.
The perturbed human hears clear instruction
so follows it—what could be simpler.

Beneath the fluid medium the men and boys
buoyant and benign obey signals serving

among school children, dreaming of bodies.
Imagine a leaf floating,
the boys below listening

(*Analysis of Newton's Method to Compute Travelling Waves in Discrete
Media*, H. J. Hupkes and Sjoerd Verduyn Lunel: "We present
a variant of Newton's method for computing travelling wave
solutions to scalar bistable lattice differential equations. We prove
that the method converges to a solution …")

to gongs, the vibrant water washing tears
away the bloom of bodies swaying to music
as to the glance of light pooling below.

The floor of the swimming pool glittery
with sun and sound, devices
divide each dancer from his dance.

Devices divide, and long afterward
humans live their lingering lives—
it is called *decay*, a straying of attention.
Nuns and mothers listen lightly.

AMONG THE FUNCTIONS OF FLOWERS

Here we would live, and near the woods
to wander after dinner. A family full
glittered in moonlight

sultry. I was one among them
and while it never happened it mattered,
"matter" as verb, a making of material

things, the lumbering into furniture and futures.
We walked on land we called
ours, and the time it took to cross it

was a lie, lovely sylvan. Tree, oak,
live (adjectival pronunciation)
there was once a place and time

in the mind of a child verdant
the child made the greenness of the time
a function of mind in the world

"world" a function involving a variable
a making required a given—the child
was given weather and a live oak profligate

of acorns. Own something small
is the advice I give.
When the Buddha walked on the earth

he left lotuses
as footprints.

Violets were sacred to Ares and Io.
The mother of Nichiren became pregnant
from dreaming of sun shining on a lotus.

ALEATORY AGILITIES

How warm the weather how cold
the cause—the clever boys are playing;
against the odds the evening comes
upon them

maybe me, among the floral
appendages, down among the dreary
rooted dotted mint and bergamot some

kind of cage to live in, clouds above
and below clods to tread; a game
of remember the river, the boys
ride home

or I rode home, did, then, when
the visit was over, the cousins washing
the dishes now, talking about us
but we cross rivers returning

sleepy, restless, useless boys
time travellers all; into the future
at a rate to allow observation
in real time;

the games begun the compass plant
and spiderwort trampled

there's no going back. Oh inconspicuous.
Oh me. The annals of Tacitus tell me
all I know of the age I live. In.
A storm is on the way.

*

The way a storm is, is inconceivable
collecting itself over time and landscape

then releasing a laughter of entropy,
energy as if

a question were asked. The answer involves
wind and water, always. And dust.
(In three dimensions there are five
regular solids; in four dimensions
six. A storm of disturbance.)

I am breathing in spite of the air
moving past me — but I cannot
not breathe and remain myself.
Is it I who breathe?

A storm in each lung, a disturbance
a havoc. *Crier havot*.

*

I asked him What do you
value most and his answer was,
Silence. Or, his answer was silence.
I cannot recall which.
I am aware that all things lie
hidden within clouds of things.
A storm is a cloud of things
and hides within itself a tumult
of time, times, brain-like. The boy
lingered too long in weather
watching the approach then
had to hurry home, chased
by the wind and various phased
waters — hail and rain and tears.

BY HEART

There is the strange case of the angle 3pi/7 (540/7 degrees). This angle cannot be constructed. But (if you managed to miraculously have it before you) it can be trisected.   Honsberger 1991, Jim Loy

Imagine a place a present tense
peopled securely by those who love
each other not you. Easily heard.

The herds of flowers bloom the birds
in feuds and foibles caught. Squirrels damage
whatever is at hand, home.

Otherwise you live wherever and read
the afternoons away. Someone told you
about the ancient problems,

the angle needs dividing, the square
wants doubling. Still, the trace
of what was lingers. Little irksome

place of origin. Folded paper.
Floral or forensic, a way of knowing
and rehearsing: rake over the coals

hoping for sparks, benign burning.
There, restricted by paper we trisect
any angle, simple, a child

can do it. Happy home
memorized, memorial to little
fingers' fierce regard.

TO YOU, IN LIEU OF

You no longer speak to me
but I will longer speak to You
beautiful as a young girl
because you are a young girl
your voice is young your face
is full of voice it is You as you
turn away your face

the voice of Youth is what
I loved first and last is why
you no longer speak to me
as if metaphor never

occurred to humans, small
and stupid as we are we never
thought of anything except the thing

we made a noise to be to be voice
only not to mean the other thing
the voice of You only means You
are there, here, where voice
arose in vibratory air the air
around me surrounds me susurrus.

*

(Arvo Pärt: *I have discovered that it is
enough when a single note is beautifully played.
This one note, or a silent beat, or
a moment of silence, comforts me*.)

When You would speak to Me
she would say things, and I would listen
and then I would speak
and this would not do.

(Dream: In line to buy tickets to a screening
I have mine the seller is You also director
of the film, I am speaking to You charming
etc. — erotics happen, I speak of movies
of *Medium Cool* to explain the line "Watch
out Haskell, it's real!" but somewhere
in the process I wake and continue the
elaboration in my now-waking mind

now I am awake and aware and continue
considering intricate sound
dubbed when it was not real
tear gas nor history there is a subplot

to dream my dream of a family
You sent me to connect.
But you would not tell me the tears
were real You who alone would know.)

*

I am but a small noise I have several noises in me   (T. Tzara)

*

there must be brain mechanisms that act
to distinguish self-generated mental experiences
(arising from neural activity initiated by our own brains)
from mental experiences stimulated through our sense organs

she said or would have said she was reading
the voice was no longer coming from outside
my self but was self-generated
sad and sudden loss, knowing.

INAUDIBLE CHILD

Surely goodness and mercy et cetera
Evilchild is attested as an English surname
from the thirteenth century
Bad Boy he would say when he failed
answer   failed boy ailing   bad answer

to "have" a child   to hold   as if
he will will himself   against you and your
ambition   notice how he walks late
as possible   yet   to escape is his plan his
fond ambition

to have or heave into a future   a child
complain as you will he won't   outgrow you
he loves to leave you

the day is fair.

*

Go forth and multiply
A few birds grow into consciousness
an experiment in a lab
all science is fiction   (cf. L. *facere)*
manufacturable:
the art of numbering and measuring exactly
a thing whose existence cannot be conceived.

*

The boy you had had a mind
of his own   his owning a mind
engaged   engulfed him   how

fear flows through the mind
my daughter dared my son supposed
my twins forgave their failings

fear follows through the minding
mannerly behaviors   fearful tears
of infancy infect   A parent fails

and still wisteria flourishes
along the fence filling the child's
room with sweetness   A bee arrives

*

Any child an imaginary friend.

*

He flapped his arms as if to fly
to try   he saw what was not

he spoke silently within and watched
for signs   calm without fear   with fear
after learning to tie his shoes he soon
forgot   nor cared

Any stick produces stigma   stigmata
divine favor or folly   grace or disgrace.

*

Honey   a hive and a little balm
spices and myrrh and nuts and almonds

a land the boy would dream of
of wheat and barley and vines and fig trees
pomegranates a land of oil and olive and honey

          and bees
would visit through his windows and the sound
would soothe him into sleep the sound
like no other sound convinced him of sanctity

a land of law and visions.

and he made him to suck honey out of the rock
and oil out of the flinty rock
he made him ride on the high places of the earth

as the small rain upon the tender herb.

MIMETISM, A LOW ART

Figure, an evasion,
lives a little life and dies—of the order
Lepidoptera, let's say, or an even lesser life

an image as imitator
the pattern by which it lived, dots and stripes
to fool such fellow creatures as would eat
his like, his kind—the

sun in this
world shines late in the season, warms
the autumn a gift, a grace undeserved
but agreeable as light encourages.

Among us are humans fallen
and among us are those who say
small things, mumble messages
waiting for dark the season

welcome to our vision, yours:
model and mimic, a paired accomplishment.
Selection is natural.

*

On the other hand nothing
no thing hands the message on
like dna does. This is science.

Biological gods break hearts daily
deny, turn the child
into his own enemy self.

But I like the sun shining this way
this day, the wrong time of year the worst
yet to come. The gift on my eyelids. Of
the ability to close.

All butterflies banished, all flowers
felled by frost—still I am sitting
in my garden. As if. Human.

*

What the insects do—the stick which walks
the beetle which blends and the moth leaflike
clings to the gray limb—is make art
of themselves, all to be less noticed
or mis-taken for worth less than the trouble
it would take. I am impressed.

I have a painted eye I have
painted an eye to see through it looks
like an eye on a wing I am watched
and watching and safe as any imitation.

THE PALE GREEN LEAF CLINGS WHITE TO THE LIT NIGHT

and shakes a little on its stiff, tense twig
Robert Lowell

To see where we are we look
through limbs and branches up

for instance to watch a planet cross the disk
of the sun — Venus between us a shadow a dark

dot against the bright, moving.
I am happy to be home in sunlight, a creature

like a lizard warming at rest.

There are circles on the walls, windows
mirrors, faces of clocks.

Imagine the child balanced precarious
prayerful above a maelstrom —

make it flames (*their foot shall slide*)
and Venus crossing between us

where to fall is to embrace
gravity

thus the sun is down from every view
look down into heavens of flame

the vertigo is in the ear
a music deafens as in the movies

paranoia is a kind of practice
useful, warning.

TOO

Good to Be True

This quote "'is a sentence fragment' is
a sentence fragment" is true
and a kind of wounding of the mouth

his unhappiness theorem appeared
in papers published but small
animals still quiver, nimble neurotics

a bounded amoeba
the concentric mapping
reproduction by division, immortality

gerrymander, the rule of contiguity
(amoeba new because of lack of contiguity)
other formations of new selves

curious creatures'
main interest is the meaning
of their own existence;

the child is neither her mother
nor her father nor both nor neither
but is not a new thing in the universe

the Higgs boson is
is part of all has always been;
tooth, claw, thorn, beak

break skin, bring blood
into the light the light
cannot be held in the hands

but can be held in the hands
the light once shone on stone
while I looked—water, a stream

streamed above enlighted
stones diffracted. I put one
broken stone in the sun

one hand in the water to clean
the hand of small blood
where is little, nothing, more.

Small a Prayer to Answer

The new holiness engages without harm
or help; hereafter regain your footing
on your own, small boy; never ask again.
In the new music the old forms flounder,

hear it in the mandolins, the men bent
embellishing old notes as they go —
they call it prayer these days. They call
upon the freshest gods, the ones behind

the new cloud formations behind the old
foothills. Some of us know better than
to build the free-form cathedrals being

called for, the undergrounds, the bomb
shelters. Still, it is a way to be, to be
good, isn't it; to make sure or safe the young.

Political an Atmosphere

I look up and see no stars.
I find I am afraid.
I follow fear into silence.

Comfort is coming.

A complication comforts,
extends tendrils into the brain
the basal ganglia:

Forget it, the child would say
when asked for clarity.
Oblivion. I find fear
A form of forgetting.

The collapsible solace.

I find I am of those wanderers,
plankton, small whale-loved feeders
nosing a way along as if

anything could be said directly:
for instance, I love you. For
instance, This is a world of
difference, a planet.

Interplanetary scintillation
is *when radio waves travel through*
fluctuations in the density of the electrons and
protons that make up the solar wind. What

can it mean to say *"The winds*
are supersonic"? Who has ears to hear
the solar wind?

Hot for Sleeping

I am living through a season of heat
and drought, weeks at a time I live,
like Ptolemy, observing myself observing
solar winds and weather, withering

looking through the air at night
makes stars twinkle. No two observers see
the same twinkle, though they see
the same stars. It is a dance

light dances because we breathe. No,
not because, but related: we look
and we breathe and we move
and we wait for rain, for the return
of that which is worth fearing.
Worth revering.

WHY IT IS PAINFUL TO SPEAK

"The ideograph for 'to speak' is
a mouth with two words and a flame" (Fenellosa)

If I say "my back is killing me" then who am I,
not my back, or must I say I am killing me.
Some things can be said for instance Hello
please accompany me to the examination room.
And some cannot.
The word for happiness is a smile with pigeon
volant
The word for wordlessness is a wind with
thistles
The word for worldlessness is a wind
The word for agony is agony
The word for agony is an open hand
Some words remind me of the boats
of my childhood the shine
the shine and a slightly orange
glow under the sun from the deck
of an uncle's open boat when he took
me into the Gulf of Mexico
The word for blessed is an east wind
scintillant and redolent
The word for give is a dog's tongue in sunlight
The word for sparrow is sparrow
The word for caution is two squares
superimposed

I translate myself into myself—
sane phrases, words and words
Returning into Sabine Bay we would
stare forward into a horizon the dark
smear of cypress and palmetto not
yet arisen to separate sky from water
the shape of the boat a word

well pronounced
necessary and variable signifying alike
a kind of health or youth.

Calligraphy is consolation.
How the snow first clears the space
of ground on the ground a gesture
marks tracks then covers them:
letter word blank time
walking is a gestural art
shoveling snow a pleasure
of sorts, painful as the pattern progresses.
The pattern of snow on a sidewalk
imagined, managed. A hand made message.

THE SECOND MOST IMPORTANT LIVING GODDESS
CALLED KUMARI UNDER THE MOON

The word "goddess" can be filled
with flesh but not blood.
The current Kumari Devi lives in Patan,
has been a goddess for six years
and may at any moment lose
divinity to menarche. Anomalies of godly
ambitions fill every poet's thoughts because
the word is the world, as well.
Every child a saint, every sin a game.

Love all the words but mostly
live with worn ones, lost
enfeebled gestures like "pear"
into "pare" and "pair." I mean
like "mean" and meanness,
even medium. Like shadowy
shopping carts push them around
and fill them up—filled with shadows
of intention, with anxious
admonishment, a poem. Shade.

Lucretius loved Epicurus, knew
the world through him. This
meaning is clear: love is a way
of knowing, of assuming the known.

                    *

To know is to narrate.
People die trying to tell what
it was like there then. Others
die of not trying. The form of this
telling is, for example,
a trellis. A growth controlled
unpredictable within measure.

Trellis. *Tri licium*. Three threads.
The weaver knows
through the fingers the way worlds
hold together. Basket makers.
The shadow of a trellis is filled
against itself, against measure.
See the sun try again to

equal the movement of the rose
climbing among the woven ways.

There flowed the flowing water

"We know of no parallel, or even an analogue, to this.
In fact it can hardly be regarded as a game."   (*Studies in Cheremis*)

The children arrange themselves in a line facing forward.
The end child runs quickly to the front.
When that child arrives the new last child runs
in turn. In this way the children like flowing water
flow down the street.

The children are children the flow washes nothing away.
Tiny woundings in the wilderness of games, children
find each other and organize. Nigerian children played
a form of game they called *Omo ni mo wa ra; mi o ra eru*:
"I come to buy children; I do not buy slaves."
They moved as a chain down the street.

Now children arrange in a circle, face outward;
avoiding the predator within is harder than
avoiding the one without. Another game is
The Bee, the Arch, the Lock. Sun and Moon face
each other forming an arch with arms. Bee
leads her little bees streaming beneath
until the last bee through is captured and declares
for Sun or for Moon. Casualties accumulate. One side

wins, the other loses. This is nature. Childhood.

Fall. Things. Sudden.

To know better—

Paul on the road struck down by light was
never the same again. I crossed the street
myself to be struck by a careless driver
and after surgery was the same.

Subitize: know the number of
immediately without counting;
usually three or less, but arrangement
can enable a higher noncounting knowledge.
I never saw it coming, to count.

"*Litost* (Czech), a state of agony and torment created by
the sudden sight of one's own agony and torment"

                    *

During my first semester of college one Sunday I,
aware of the time, sat talking to a girl, wary.
I heard her voice and another within
without body. It said
I should get to church by noon but knew
I could attend a later mass. The talking
continued while hours passed then one moment
I knew I would not attend the services.

And I rather knew also I would never again
go, I who had been the best of Catholic boys,
who had never eaten meat on Friday nor
missed mass on Sunday. It was a kind
of nothing, of no consequence.
It was autumn, the best of seasons
in Baton Rouge. Livable among trellises
among live oaks among late
magnolia bloomings in the fields.

Field

If the voice can be certainly traced to a point
outside the skin the self is safe to listen. If
voice begins within, there lies danger.

If in a field he hears consolation or contrition,
if in a field she cannot see persons, any direction,
if in a field he hears voices …

instances:
Guillaume de Machaut
listened. The day went round him as he
stood. The voice (six hundred years past)
of a child who loved him.

The spoken voice must be believed
no matter its source. The body its pledge.

Voir, so long ago, not voice but truth;
say truth if you can, if you cannot
say the beautiful thing; you hear
Le voit dit. Voir dire.

The field of complex numbers is a ring.
A commutative ring. A field is image, imaginary.

1424 at the age of 12 years, Joan alone
in a field saw visions heard voices
of Saints Michael, Catherine, and Margaret.
She heard also the bronze bell of the stone church.

During a later war a certain
Canadian doctor heard birds and bullets
The larks, still bravely singing, fly   (Lt. John McCrae)
so says the voice of the dead:
(Take up our quarrel with the foe) ...

                    *

I learned not to fear infinity,
The far field, wrote Roethke, still alive,
who heard not-voices and listened
afraid or not, no matter. Fear matters.

        Names Assigned

Opposed to practice in Nepal, Indian
Kumaris are worshiped only one day
but still these names are assigned
while the ritual lasts, a matter of hours:

A one-year-old girl goddess is Sandhya,
a two-year-old is named Sarasvati,
the name of the child at three is Tridhamurti;
on her fourth birthday she is Kalika,

on her fifth Subhaga, when she is six
she becomes Uma, then
at seven she is called Malini;
an eight year girl is Kubjika;
named in her ninth year Kaalasandarbha,
upon reaching ten she is called Aparajita;
but an eleven-year-old Kumari is always Rudrani,
who on her twelfth birthday is renamed Bhairavi,
then at thirteen she is Mahalakshmi,
at fourteen Pithanayika.
If at fifteen she is still prepubescent
she is called Kshetragya; at sixteen years
of her age she has attained the name Ambika.

Only the rarest remain a Kumari at sixteen
since nobility replaces divinity; this world not that.
What else can be named, Love?

*

Chandrayaan-1 was the name
of the moon mission launched October 2008
by the Indian Space Research Organization
to look for water (molecules of which
it found in the dust of the lunar surface).

There are no rivers on the moon. India
did not need to spend sixty million dollars
to know that, but it was worth it
to learn that the ghost, the faintest ghost
of a river, can be found under its dust.

The moon as our sister we knew always
had a shadow, a hint, a breath of River
in a secret repertoire.

Between earth and moon is a bridge
sometimes whose molecules
we hold in common, water or its shadow,
the shadow of water, its thinness next
to nothing, unnamed both there and here.

INTRICATE PICNIC

Embarrassed by hunger
the birds feed and yet
they notice the world falling tattered;
they notice the moon is
small enough to fit curled in a nest.

A Le Conte's sparrow, one of three hundred
fifty-five banded and never
recovered. A quarrel of sparrows. An entire
crew lost. A ubiquity never seen again.
A flutter, and then flight.

                    *

My brother would read
from my poems, would recite
in gardens, in parks in the days
when "paradise" and "garden"
invoked enclosure, secrecy, defense;

he walked at evening shrouded by mosquitoes
a punctuation of flesh.
He heard their whine as warning:
full bodies to blood fly, fierce;
little creatures we are, too, defenseless
nestled, nestling infestation of self
within self. Dream some evening
in a garden going to seed, late

shelter to the lesser beings, the flying—
flies and bees, bumbled, burdened
creatures of the pollen. The garden shelter

—we walk

with various gods and fears in the evening
surrounded by breath, words, whining wings.
Old mistakes, made often enough, become
a kind of wisdom; go figure.

ACKNOWLEDGMENTS

Several of the poems in this book were published previously, often in different forms:

Bombay Gin: "In Late Evening the Light Overseen," "Population Genetics"

Chronicle of Higher Education: "Hausdorff Spaces"

Diode: "Litmus," "A Random Walk (Central Limit Theorem)," "Going Without, Saying"

Fence: "The Pale Green Leaf Clings White to the Lit Night," "The Chemical Basis of Morphogenesis"

The Gulf Stream: "Resonance," "Among the Functions of Flowers," "Aleatory Agilities"

Harvey Hix, *www.hlhix.com/inquire/*: "Mattering"

Lana Turner: "Happy Is He Who Has Discovered the Causes of Things," "A Molecular Vision Clouded," "Rule of Double False Position" and "Traditional Future: A Tense"

The Laurel Review: "My Private Periodic Table" as "A Self an Affinity Table"

New American Writing: "Too," "Why It Is Painful to Speak"

Poets.org, *Poem-A-Day* (10/24/12): "Curve of Pursuit"

NOTES

Several quoted phrases are from others' published works:

"weaponized pastoral," repopularized by the TV series "Elementary," originally from *My Adventures as a Spy* (1915) by Robert Baden-Powell, founder of the Boy Scouts

"Happy is he who has discovered the causes of things" from Virgil's *Georgics*, Book II

"The Chemical Basis of Morphogenesis," from Alan Turing's article of the same name

"The pale green leaf clings white to the lit night," from Robert Lowell's "Through the Night"

"Happy the hare at morning, for she cannot read / The Hunter's [...]" from W. H. Auden's "The Dog Beneath the Skin"

"random walk," a term in statistics introduced by Karl Pearson, a protégé of Francis Galton

"just and gentle plans" from Hesiod's *Theogony*

Bin Ramke's first book won the Yale
Younger Poets Award in 1979; *Missing
the Moon* is his twelfth. He teaches at
the University of Denver where he
holds the Phipps Chair in English and
where he edited the *Denver Quarterly*
for seventeen years. He teaches on fall
terms at the School of the Art Institute
of Chicago. He edited over eighty
books of poems for the University of
Georgia Press.

Missing the Moon
by Bin Ramke

Cover & Interior text set Didot LT Std & ITC Avant Garde Gothic STD

Cover photo courtesy of NASA photo archive

Book cover and interior design by Peter Burghardt

Offset printed in the United States
by Edwards Brothers Malloy, Ann Arbor, Michigan
On 55# Enviro Natural 100% Recycled 100% PCW
Acid Free Archival Quality FSC Certified Paper
with Rainbow FSC Certified Colored End Papers

Omnidawn Publishing
Richmond, California
2014
Rusty Morrison & Ken Keegan, Senior Editors & Publishers
Gillian Hamel, Managing Poetry Editor & OmniVerse Managing Editor
Cassandra Smith, Poetry Editor & Book Designer
Peter Burghardt, Poetry Editor & Book Designer
Turner Canty, Poetry Editor
Liza Flum, Poetry Editor & Social Media
Sharon Osmond, Poetry Editor & Bookstore Outreach
Pepper Luboff, Poetry Editor & Feature Writer
Juliana Paslay, Fiction Editor & Bookstore Outreach Manager
Gail Aronson, Fiction Editor
RJ Ingram, Social Media
Melissa Burke, Poetry Editor & Feature Writer
Sharon Zetter, Grant Writer & Poetry Editor